Family Life

4

STUDENT EDITION

David Thomas, PhD

General Editor

RCL✷ Benziger®

Cincinnati, Ohio

Consultants

Paul Duckro, PhD
Tim Hogan, PsyD
Tom Everson
Fanny Pedraza

NIHIL OBSTAT
Rev. Msgr. Robert Coerver
Censor Librorum

IMPRIMATUR
† Most Reverend Kevin J. Farrell DD
Bishop of Dallas

May 3, 2010

The *Nihil Obstat* and *Imprimatur* are official declarations that the material reviewed is free of doctrinal or moral error. No implication is contained therein that those granting the *Nihil Obstat* and *Imprimatur* agree with the contents, opinions, or statements expressed.

RCL Benziger Development Team

James Spurgin
Editor

Tricia Legault
Design

Laura Fremder
Production

Daniel S. Mulhall
National Catechetical Advisor

Jo Rotunno
Director of Catechist and Professional Development

Susan Smith
Director of Project Development

Ed DeStefano
Publisher

Peter M. Esposito
President

ACKNOWLEDGMENTS

Excerpts from the *New American Bible* with Revised New Testament and Revised Psalms © 1991, 1986, 1970 Confraternity of Christian Doctrine, Washington, D.C. and are used by permission of the copyright owner. All Rights Reserved. No part of the New American Bible may be reproduced in any form without permission in writing from the copyright owner.

Excerpts from *Catholic Household Blessings and Prayers*, copyright © 2007, United States Conference of Catholic Bishops, Washington, D.C. All rights reserved.

PHOTO CREDITS

Cover, Olga Lyubkina/iStock; Page 6, Jupiterimages/Gettyimages; 8, Corbis/Punchstock; 9, Francis Hammond/Gettyimages; 9, Photo Researchers Inc.; 10, David Buffington/Gettyimages; 11, Masterfile - ebk; 12, Age Fotostock America/Age Fotostock; 12, Alison Barnes Martin/Masterfile - ebk; 12, Romme/Masterfile - ebk; 14, David Papazian/Masterfile - ebk; 15, Photo Network/Alamy; 16, Comstock/Gettyimages; 16, Alex Wong/Gettyimages; 21, SuperStock; 22, Masterfile-17/Masterfile - ebk; 23, Josh Hodge/iStock; 24, Rosemarie Gearhart/iStock; 27, Mira/Alamy; 28, Tom Grill/Gettyimages; 34, Kevin Dodge/Masterfile - ebk; 35, Mike Bluestone/Alamy; 36, Jupiterimages/Gettyimages; 39, Karin Dreyer/Gettyimages; 39, LWA/Gettyimages; 39, Jani Byrson/iStock; 40, Jupiterimages/Gettyimages; 41, Brandon Laufenberg/iStock; 42, Jose More/AP Images; 45, Bridgeman Art Library/Bridgeman Art; 47, Photo Researchers Inc.; 47, Photo Researchers Inc.; 47, Photo Researchers Inc.; 48, David Oxberry/Gettyimages; 50, Gene Plaisted/The Crosiers; 51, ERproductions Ltd/Blend/Gettyimages; 52, USDA; 54, Getty Images/Gettyimages; 57, Bettmann/Corbis; 58, BananaStock/Fotosearch; 59, Toby Maudsley/Gettyimages; 60, Ariel Skelley/Corbis; 62, Tim Graham/Alamy; 63, Archdiocese of Detroit/AP Images

CONTENTS

The Catholic Home

Unit 1: God's Gift of Family

Unit 2: God's Gift of Self

Unit 3: God's Gift of Life

Unit 4: God's Gift of Love

Unit 5: God's Gift of Community

Reviewing Grade 4

The Catholic Home

Life in Christ

In Baptism you have been called to share in the life of Christ. You have been given a great gift, but the gift requires that you give your best effort to follow Christ. This means that you need to learn the difference between right and wrong and choose to do what is right and good. When you learn to choose to do what is right, you are leading a life in Christ.

The following list will help you review how to lead a life in Christ. Almost everything you will learn this year has been designed to help you and your family love your way through life, by following the way of Jesus. In these ways, you can share a family life in Christ:

1. **You have been created in the image and likeness of God.** This truth is the starting point for Christian living in a Catholic home.

2. **You are called to do what is good.** The Ten Commandments and the Beatitudes tell you that God calls you to live a healthy, holy, and happy life. Being weakened by the effects of Original Sin makes doing what is good difficult. With God's grace you can choose good.

3. **You are created to be happy.** You have a natural desire to be happy. The Church teaches that when you know, love, and serve God, you can be truly happy.

4. **You are created free.** You have the gift of free will. This makes it possible to choose how to live and to act. Yet God calls you to be responsible for your actions.

5. **You have a conscience.** You have the ability to know the difference between what is right and what is wrong. This judgment is called *conscience*. The Sacred Scriptures, the teachings of the Church, and the examples of good people help you to inform and form your conscience and to follow it.

6. **You have been given the gifts of the virtues.** At your Baptism, you were given the gifts of faith, hope, and love. These Theological Virtues help you to develop all the good habits you need to live in Christ. With God's grace, you can live according to the virtues.

7. **The Holy Spirit helps you lead a good life.** Jesus sent his Spirit into the world to help people, including you, to lead a healthy, holy, and happy life.

8. **God is merciful.** God gives the gift of mercy to all those who are sorry for their sins, receive the Sacraments, and strive to do what is good. Though when we sin, we fail to love God and others, with God's merciful and forgiving love, we can change our ways.

9. **You have a responsibility to the human community.** You have been made to live in community. You are called to help society live according to the way of Jesus.

10. **You follow legitimate authority.** Inspired by the Holy Spirit, the Church helps you learn about Christian living. You can follow the authority of the Pope and the bishops. You can also follow the just rules of society. And most importantly, you can obey your parents too.

11. **You have the Ten Commandments and the Beatitudes as your guide.** Learning to follow the Ten Commandments and to live in the spirit of the Beatitudes will help you love your way through a life in Christ.

12. **You know and follow the Law of Love.** In everything you do, you want to show that you love God with your whole heart and that you love your neighbor as yourself.

Prayers for the Family

The Sign of the Cross

In the name of the Father,
and of the Son,
and of the Holy Spirit. Amen.

Glory Be

Glory be to the Father
and to the Son
and to the Holy Spirit,
as it was in the beginning
is now, and ever shall be
world without end.
Amen.

The Lord's Prayer

Our Father, who art in heaven,
hallowed be thy name;
thy kingdom come,
thy will be done
on earth as it is in heaven.
Give us this day our daily bread,
and forgive us our trespasses,
as we forgive those who
   trespass against us;
and lead us not into temptation,
   but deliver us from evil. Amen.

The Hail Mary

Hail, Mary, full of grace,
the Lord is with thee.
Blessed art thou among women
and blessed is the fruit
   of thy womb, Jesus.
Holy Mary, Mother of God,
pray for us sinners,
now and at the hour of our death.
Amen.

Prayer to the Holy Spirit

Come, Holy Spirit, fill the hearts of your faithful.
And kindle in them the fire of your love.
Send forth your Spirit and they shall be created.
And you will renew the face of the earth.

Lord,
by the light of the Holy Spirit
you have taught the hearts of your faithful.
In the same Spirit
help us to relish what is right
and always rejoice in your consolation.
We ask this through Christ our Lord. Amen.

Morning Prayer

Almighty God, you have given us this day. Strengthen us with your power and keep us from falling into sin. May whatever we say or think or do be in your service, and for the sake of your kingdom. Amen.

Evening Prayer

Lord, watch over us this night.
By your strength, may we rise
    at daybreak to rejoice
in the Resurrection of Christ, your Son,
who lives and reigns for ever and ever.
Amen.

Grace Before Meals

Bless us, O Lord,
and these thy gifts,
which we are about to receive
from thy bounty,
through Christ our Lord. Amen.

Grace After Meals

We give thee thanks, for all thy benefits, almighty God, who lives and reigns forever. Amen.

A Prayer for Forgiveness

My God, I am sorry for my sins with all my heart. In choosing to do wrong and failing to do good, I have sinned against you whom I should love above all things. I firmly intend, with your help, to do penance, to sin no more, and to avoid whatever leads me to sin. Our Savior Jesus Christ suffered and died for us. In his name, my God, have mercy. Amen.

A Vocation Prayer

God our Father, it is your will that all people be saved and come to the knowledge of the truth. Send workers into your great harvest that the Gospel might be preached to every person, and that your people, gathered together by the Word of Life and strengthened by the power of the Sacraments, may advance in the way of salvation and love. Grant this through Christ our Lord. Amen.

Family Prayer

Heavenly Father, you have given us a beautiful example in the Holy Family of Jesus, Mary, and Joseph. Give us openness to your Spirit, so that we may follow through in the family practice of virtues. Strengthen our bonds of love. Grant us the courage to reach out to those in need and to do your will. Amen.

Family Living

The Great Commandment

"You shall love the Lord, your God, with all your heart,
with all your soul, and with all your mind. . . .
You shall love your neighbor as yourself."   Matthew 22:37–39

Jesus' Commandment

"This is my commandment:
love one another as I love you."

John 15:12

The Ten Commandments

1. I am the LORD your God: you shall not have strange gods before me.
2. You shall not take the name of the LORD your God in vain.
3. Remember to keep holy the LORD's Day.
4. Honor your father and your mother.
5. You shall not kill.
6. You shall not commit adultery.
7. You shall not steal.
8. You shall not lie.
9. You shall not covet your neighbor's wife.
10. You shall not covet your neighbor's goods.

Based on Exodus 20:2–3, 7–17

The Beatitudes

Blessed are the poor in spirit,
    for theirs is the kingdom of heaven.
Blessed are they who mourn,
    for they will be comforted.
Blessed are the meek,
    for they will inherit the land.
Blessed are they who hunger
        and thirst for righteousness,
    for they will be satisfied.
Blessed are the merciful,
    for they will be shown mercy.
Blessed are the clean of heart,
    for they will see God.
Blessed are the peacemakers,
    for they will be called children of God.
Blessed are they who are persecuted
        for the sake of righteousness,
    for theirs is the kingdom of heaven.

Matthew 5:3–10

The Theological Virtues
Faith, Hope and Love

The Cardinal Virtues
Justice, Fortitude,
Temperance, Prudence

Family Time

Family Responsibilities and Rules

God created us to live in communion with him. We are members of the family of God—the Church. We live in a family, a neighborhood, a town or city, and a country. We are discovering more and more that we are also part of a global family.

Our family is the first and most important family God created us to belong to. Members of a family have responsibilities toward one another—children toward parents and parents toward children. Family members have the rightful expectation that they can depend on one another—in good times and in bad times, in times of joy and in times of sadness. Meeting our responsibilities as members of the family in a dependable and consistent manner is an expression of the depth of our love and respect for our family.

Family rules help us show our love and respect for one another. All good family rules flow from and are an expression of God's rules. God's rules are part of who we are. They have been clearly revealed to us by Jesus Christ and taught to us by the Church. All good family rules help family members live together as God created us to do.

Family Blessings

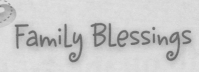

Take time together for prayer. Ask God to continually bless your family with the patience and determination to live according to his rules.

Healthy Habits in the Home

Involve your child in making some of your family's rules. Consider the family chores. Be sure your family's list of chores meets the needs of the whole family.

Taking the Lesson Home

Read and think about the traits of a holy and healthy family. Choose one of these traits and work on it.

A healthy and holy family . . .

1. communicates and listens.
2. affirms and supports.
3. shows and teaches respect for others.
4. develops a sense of trust.
5. laughs and has a sense of play.
6. shares responsibilities.
7. teaches a sense of right and wrong.
8. enjoys rituals and traditions.
9. includes every family member.
10. has faith in God.

Making Connections

Family members show one another love and respect by helping each other out, as Ricky does in the story in lesson 1, and by following family rules, as Teresa learns in the story in lesson 2. Spend time as a family sharing responses to these questions:

▶ How well can our family depend on me?
▶ How do we show appreciation for what we do for one another?
▶ What are some important rules our family lives by?
▶ How does obeying and following those rules help our family be more loving?

Faith on the Fridge

God said to honor your father and mother. In giving honor, you receive love. This is God's plan for families. Parents are to love their children. Children are to love and honor their parents. To better appreciate God's gift of family, parents and children are to grow in the virtue of justice through obedience and self-giving.

Family Web Time
RCLBFamilyLife.com

Being Needed

Ricky to the Rescue

Ricky's mother was lying on the sofa with a white cast on her right arm. Two green pillows propped up her arm to help reduce the swelling. The day before, she tripped on a broken porch step, fell and broke a bone in her arm.

"I need your help," Mom told Ricky. "I'll be depending on you for a few weeks now. I'd like for you to cook dinner for us. Jack and Linda will be home in time to help with the cleaning afterwards."

Ricky scratched his head. He was confused. His own mother, "Super Mom," was asking for his help! Ricky saw the look of pain on her face. She really needed him!

"No problem, Mom," said Ricky. "Cooking dinner might be fun!"

"Right now, I have to rest. Everything you need is in the kitchen," Mom assured Ricky. "Call me if you need some help."

As his mother shut her eyes, Ricky went to the kitchen. She had put out all the things with instructions on making a hamburger casserole and rolls. At 5 P.M., Ricky slid the casserole and rolls into the oven. The kitchen was a bit messy, but dinner would be a feast!

Ricky felt proud. He was glad that his mother was willing to depend on him. Ricky slipped outside to play basketball for a few minutes. He sank basket after basket. Then he heard Jack and Linda come up behind him.

"Nice basket!" Linda said. "You're a hot shot!" Jack said.

"Yeah," Ricky said smiling, "out here and in the kitchen, too!"

> **This lesson will help you to:**
> - **explore** the importance of being someone your family can depend on.
> - **discover** ways to be a responsible member of your family.
> - **make** choices to show your family that they can depend on you.

 How can you show responsibility to your family?

Catholics Believe

God created us in his image and likeness. He created us to live in communion with him and with one another.

I Depend on You

"I need your help." These are words used in every family. Husbands and wives say them to each other. Children say them to their parents, and parents say them to their children. You depend on your family, and your family depends on you.

 Think about some of the many ways that you depend on your family.

There are many things you need that you cannot provide for yourself, like food, clothing, and a place to live. You need check-ups from doctors in order to stay healthy. You need teachers to help you learn about the world. Most importantly, you need your family to keep you safe and to help you grow in love and faith.

You depend upon others for things that money cannot buy. Your family helps you fulfill these needs. Family members give you love. They give you encouragement when you try to do difficult things. Loving family members also provide guidance. That means that they give you good advice when you are not sure what to do. Sometimes you are faced with difficult decisions. When this happens, members in your family can give you guidance to help you determine what the right choice is.

Our Church family needs each of us as well. We support and pray for one another. At Mass we need everyone to participate in order to best praise and thank God for the gifts he has given to us.

Your family depends on you. They trust that you will be responsible and that they can depend on you not only at home, but in other places too. You show responsibility and dependability at school, at your friend's home, and at church. Being responsible to your family and friends shows that they can depend on you to meet your obligations to them.

When you act this way, you practice the virtue of justice. You honor your parents and demonstrate your love for them by doing what they ask. You show that others can depend on you by giving your time and talents to help someone else. Perhaps someone in your family just needs you to be there with them for support.

Helping and being helped depends on love. When we give and receive love, we become better persons and a stronger family closer to God.

Growing in Virtue

Justice is the virtue that strengthens us to act responsibly and give to others what is due to them—what is their right—or making sure they have what they need.

"Being Dependable"

Complete the chart by naming ways you can show each group how they can depend on you.

Family Members	Classmates	Friends

Catholic Family Album

Saint Elizabeth Ann Seton was born in the United States in 1774 right before the Revolutionary War. When her husband died, she was left to raise five children on her own. To help raise her children, she became a teacher. She later started the first Catholic school in the United States. After her own children grew up, Elizabeth began a community of religious sisters. She showed her responsibility for her own family and many others too.

Giving of Self

As you grow, you are learning how to grow in love. You come to see that loving includes both giving and receiving. When you give of your time and talents for the benefit of someone else, you demonstrate self-giving love.

You are growing in love, as well as in height. When you are dependable and responsible, you are growing in love. Answering these questions can help you make a decision to grow in self-giving love.

1. When did I see someone in my family in need?

_____

_____

_____

_____

_____

_____

2. What will I do to show my family that they can depend on me?

When someone is _____ , I will _____

_____ .

When someone is _____ , I will _____

_____ .

When someone is _____ , I will _____

_____ .

Why Rules?

I See What You Mean

Teresa Sanchez giggled. What great fun she had after school. She and five other girls played soccer at the vacant lot on Meade Street. Teresa was very sweaty, but happy. She ran several blocks home and then up the stairs two at a time. Teresa fished for her key in her book bag. She let herself in.

"Where have you been, Teresa?" asked her father from the kitchen.

Surprised, Teresa dropped her book bag. Her dad was home. She expected the apartment to be empty. Suddenly, she realized what was wrong. She had broken a Sanchez family rule. One of the family rules was that the children were to come straight home after school unless they had permission to do something else. This was a family safety rule.

"Why didn't you come home right after school?" her dad asked. "You know that's the rule."

Teresa looked up at her father. His forehead was wrinkled. He looked pretty worried! "I forgot," she said quietly. "I played soccer."

"Your mother was worried too, Teresa," he said. "She had to go to work. She called me to come home from the garage. Your brothers are out looking for you. You know we worry if you don't come right home," he said.

"I know," said Teresa. "I'm sorry. I got caught up playing soccer."

"Teresa," her father said, gently laying his hand on her shoulder. "I've been working on a car that was wrecked in a traffic accident. Often, people are hurt when someone doesn't obey a traffic rule. Rules are made to protect us. This family rule is to help protect you. We want you to always be safe."

"Okay, Dad," Teresa said. "I see what you mean."

This lesson will help you to:
- **explore** the importance of rules in your family.
- **discover** ways to keep your family's rules.
- **make** choices to obey your family's rules.

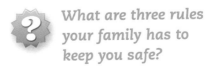
What are three rules your family has to keep you safe?

Catholics Believe

Obeying good rules shows our respect, honor, and love for our parents, the Church, our teachers, and other people who have a responsibility to help us live by God's rules.

Family Rules

There seem to be so many rules! There are rules at school, at home, and at church. Some of these rules tell you, "Don't do this" or "Don't do that." Sometimes, hearing so many "don'ts" is hard. You might forget that there are important reasons for having rules. You might even think that some rules are silly or do not make sense.

Little rules help you to follow bigger rules. Making your bed may seem like a waste of time. But following that rule is a way of both taking care of what has been given to you and keeping your home in order. Some big rules come from those responsible for the well-being of others, such as the government and your school. Even bigger rules come from your parents and the Church. The biggest rules come from God, such as the Ten Commandments and the Beatitudes. All good rules help us follow God's rules.

 Think about some "big" rules a family might have.

God gave each of us a wonderful gift—the gift of free will. This means that you can choose to do good and not to do evil. When you choose to obey God's Laws, his rules, you do a good act, such as an act of virtue. Yet you can choose to do something that is against God's Laws and is wrong. When you know that the act you choose to do is wrong, against God's Laws, and you still choose to do it, you commit a sin. When you sin, you are disobeying God's rules. God created rules for our benefit. When we obey God's Laws, we do what is good and right.

Learning how to make the right choice to obey good rules takes time and guidance from others. We can learn from our failures and mistakes. We can learn from others, such as the Saints, who lived the virtues. Virtues are good habits that help us live healthy and holy lives. The Church, teachers, family, and trusted friends can show us that following good rules is important. These people can teach us how obeying God's rules makes us happier and closer to God.

Growing in Virtue

Obedience is the virtue that strengthens us to grow in honor and respect for God, our parents, and other people who have the responsibility to care for us.

"Living With and Without Rules"

Write a short story or draw a picture describing what your classroom would look like if everyone did not follow the rules. Then discuss how rules can help make the classroom a better place to learn and have fun.

Catholic Family Album

Saint Benedict of Nursia and his twin sister, **Saint Scholastica**, lived in Italy around A.D. 480. As a grown-up, Benedict set up schools for children and monasteries for adults. Monasteries are places where Christian adults live together as a family to live the Gospel. Benedict wrote a book of rules called *The Rule of Saint Benedict*. These rules help people to live simply while following Jesus' teachings. *The Rule of Saint Benedict* is filled with the spirit of family and hospitality.

Choosing to Obey

"Should I wear a sweater or a jacket?" Some choices that you make are not very important. Unless you are required to wear a sweater, it might not really matter what you decide to wear.

Some choices and decisions you make are more important than others. A choice is important when it means you will obey or disobey a family rule or one of God's Commandments. A choice is also important when it affects someone, such as yourself or another. A choice can be important when the decision you make may help you or another to be a better person. Making the choice to obey God's rules and all good rules is a very important decision.

1. Name one important rule your family has:
   No going outside after midnight to 6

2. Why is it important for you to obey that family rule?
   it is important, because bad things happen at that time

3. What do you need to do to obey that family rule?
   Don't go outside after 12

4. What will you do to obey that family rule?
   Not go outside after dark.

Name ....

Summary

Remember what you have learned in each of the lessons in God's Gift of Family.

LESSON 1: Being Needed

- Family members depend on one another and bring each other closer to God.
- Being dependable to my family and friends shows my love to them.
- I live the virtue of justice when I give of myself for the needs of my family and others.

LESSON 2: Why Rules?

- Good rules help us live happy and holy lives.
- We use the gift of free will to choose to obey good rules.
- We live the virtue of obedience when we choose to follow good rules.

Thinking It Through

1. Complete the sentence by providing three different answers.

   I show that my family can depend on me when I

   a. _don't lie_
   b. _I do my homework_
   c. _I respect them_

2. Which family rules do you think are the most important?

   No going outside after midnight to 6.

3. What new family rule would you make?

   No d-pds after 9.

4. How will living that family rule help your family?

   Until the d-pds are not helpful.

Matching It Up

On each line, write the letter of the description in Column B that best goes with the term in Column A.

A

1. __B__ Self-giving love
2. __B__ Justice
3. __C__ Obedience
4. __A__ Virtues
5. __D__ Guidance

B

A. Good habits that help us live healthy and holy lives

B. The virtue that strengthens us to meet our obligations and give others what is due to them

C. The virtue that strengthens us to choose to follow good rules

D. The help and support people give to others to help them make good choices

E. To give of your time and talents for the benefit of someone else

Name...

Recalling Key Concepts

Circle the T if the statement is true. Circle the F if the statement is false.

1. You can learn through others, on your own, and through your mistakes.   (T)   F
2. The biggest rules that we are to obey come from the government.   T   (F)
3. Freedom and rules can go hand in hand.   (T)   F
4. Giving of your time and talents for someone else demonstrates love.   (T)   F
5. Every decision you make is equally important.   T   (F)

Fill in the missing words in these sentences.

6. You need your ~~family~~ *family* to help you grow in love and faith.

7. To give of your time and talents for someone demonstrates self-giving ...... *love* ....

8. God's gift of ~~free will~~ *free will* allows us to choose to obey God's rules.

9. Learning how to make the right ...... *choices* ...... takes time and guidance from others.

10. ~~~~ *Justice* is the responsible giving to others their due, ensuring that they have what they need.

Working Together

Create a digital family photo album. Gather photographs of your family. Be sure to include photos of grandparents, aunts, uncles, and cousins. Below each photograph, include the names of the people in the photograph. Nicknames would be fun! Enjoy the presentation with your family.

Feeling Under Pressure

We live in an age of instant and constant information. Powerful audio and visual messages pressure us to feel a certain way, act a certain way or live a certain way. Sometimes these messages can influence us to feel overwhelmed. Many of these images and messages are contrary to the Gospel and the teachings of the Catholic Church.

Jesus had feelings just like we do. He didn't hide his feelings. Sometimes, Jesus was very happy. But Jesus also felt sad when he saw people suffer. Imagine walking with Jesus through a dusty village. What do you feel as Jesus reaches out to help someone who is sick?

When we spend time with Jesus in prayer and by reading the Gospels, we can see how he showed his feelings. We can see how his feelings helped him do the work his Father sent him to do. Jesus will help us understand, listen to, and respond to our own feelings.

The Woman Who Had an Infirmity 18 Years by James Tissot (1836–1902/French)

Healthy Habits in the Home

With your family, read aloud Mark 1:35–45 from a Bible. Then think what it would be like if your family was with Jesus all day long. Talk about your time with Jesus, especially during Mass.

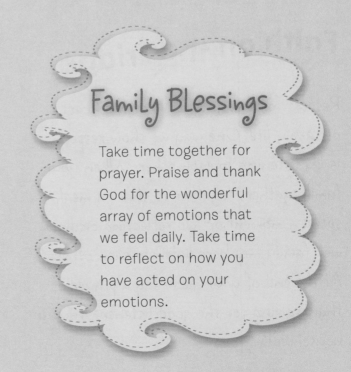

Family Blessings

Take time together for prayer. Praise and thank God for the wonderful array of emotions that we feel daily. Take time to reflect on how you have acted on your emotions.

Taking the Lesson Home

Sharing feelings appropriately takes work. Give your family a chance to do so by completing this exercise. Consider this an "emotional workout" for the family. Be honest and listen carefully. One at a time, each member completes a sentence out loud.

Continue until all sentences have been completed:

1. "I want to shout with joy when . . ."

2. "I'm very afraid of . . ."

3. "I feel sadness when . . ."

4. "I get real angry when . . ."

5. "I'm really surprised when . . ."

6. "I'm very curious about . . ."

7. "I get disgusted by . . ."

8. "I can't accept . . ."

Making Connections

Family members need to know they can honestly express their feelings within the family and will be listened to when they do. Have each member respond to the following questions and encourage everyone to listen attentively.

▶ Is it easier for you to reveal your feelings through words or through actions? How have you expressed your feelings today?

▶ Which emotion do you find most difficult to handle? How do you normally deal with that emotion?

▶ What do you believe are the most appropriate ways of expressing your emotions?

Faith on the Fridge

Respect for one another is at the heart of family life. One way we show respect is by listening to each other. When your family gathers together to share a meal, spend a moment or two reflecting on how well family members listen to each other. At the end of your meal, say a prayer of thanksgiving for the good listeners in your household!

Family Web Time
RCLBFamilyLife.com

My Feelings

Feelings on the Playground

The soccer ball bounced in front of Joey. For a moment, Joey didn't touch it. When he gave it a little kick, the ball moved only a little.

"Gee Joey!" yelled Carl as he laughed out loud. "Is that your best shot?" Carl was the best soccer player at the school.

After advancing the ball, Tony went over to Carl. "Joey's sad," Tony said softly. "His puppy was run over by a truck yesterday."

"I didn't know," Carl said.

Then the ball rolled in front of Carl. He spotted Rosa. He kicked the ball hard. It shot across the pavement and stopped at Rosa's white tennis shoes.

Carl thought Rosa was the cutest girl in the class. She was friendly to everyone. When Carl kicked the ball to her, Rosa's face lit up with joy. Carl's face turned red. He was blushing with embarrassment.

Rosa kicked the ball to her friend Jessica. Jessica had seen Rosa smile. Jessica didn't like it. Wasn't Rosa her best friend? Jessica was jealous.

Jessica kicked the ball to Tom. The ball came fast and straight at him. It hit Tom's face with a loud smack. Everyone laughed at "Poor Tom."

Tom smiled, too. But inside, he was filled with embarrassment. A girl made him look silly! He didn't like being laughed at.

Miss Anthony's whistle ended the game. "Recess is over," she said. "Let's line up for class."

This lesson will help you to:

- **explore** what feelings are and why you have them.
- **discover** why your feelings change and how to listen to and name your feelings.
- **make** the decision to let Jesus show you how best to share your feelings with others.

 How can your emotions help you make better decisions?

God gave us many kinds of emotions. Jesus has emotions, too. He is divine, but he is also human, just like us. Jesus helps us learn from our feelings. He also shows us the best ways to share our feelings with others.

Reasons for Feelings

You experience a feeling, or an emotion, as a response to something that happens to you. Feelings come from your body and mind working together. Your body gets information through your senses. Nerves send messages to your brain. Your brain responds with answers. Those answers are feelings. Some feelings are pleasant, and some are unpleasant.

What triggers your emotions? Your emotions are gifts within you that help you make decisions to do or say something. They help you react in different ways to the events in your life. You might feel excited when you get a new bike for your birthday. You could wake up startled during a terrible thunderstorm. During a long car ride home, you might feel relaxed and comfortably fall asleep on your mom's shoulder.

Other times, you have different feelings when around certain people. For example, you have a sense of excitement, joy, or spiritedness with your teammates after winning a game. Or you feel hurt or disappointed inside if the team lost. Maybe you have had a bad day and you know that a certain friend always cheers you up. You feel good about yourself when others help you see God's goodness and love.

How has someone you know helped you see God's goodness and love? What feelings did you experience?

Some feelings are hard to understand. Boys and girls your age might feel uncomfortable around each other. That will change. In the years to come, your body will undergo many changes. Slowly, over time, you will find yourself wanting to be with or even close to someone of the other, or complementary, sex.

Being close to others is important in God's plan for us. God created us to live with others. For example, in God's plan for married life, children are created through the shared love of a husband and wife.

"A Rainbow of Emotions"

In the space provided, draw and color a rainbow. On each color, write a feeling you think the color might symbolize. Then, choose one of the feelings and think about a time when you have experienced it. Write about that time inside the rainbow.

Growing in Virtue

Fortitude gives us the strength to do what is right. Courage is another name for fortitude. For example, we can practice the virtue of fortitude when we see someone being bullied on the playground. Fortitude helps us stand up for that person. It helps us make the right choice!

Catholic Family Album

Saint Philip Neri had the very special gift to make people smile and laugh. A bell rang. Children and grown-ups looked toward the sound. Their eyes brightened as they saw who was coming into their Italian village. They recognized the smiling face— it was Father Philip Neri. How he made them laugh! He was full of jokes and always ready for fun. Sometimes he wore big baggy clothes. Other times, he sang and told riddles. Saint Philip's own feeling of joy brought happiness to others. He helped people see that following Jesus is not a gloomy thing, but a thing of joy.

Acting on Your Feelings

Each feeling you have can help you choose to do something good. It is important to ask yourself, "What am I feeling, and why am I feeling this way?" Naming a feeling you are having helps you to listen to it, understand it, learn from it and act on it appropriately.

Imagine yourself experiencing each of the events below. Complete the sentences to help you listen to and act on your feelings.

1. Today is your birthday. Your family has planned a celebration. Some cousins and friends are waiting for you. You didn't know they were coming. You arrive and . . .

   In this moment, I feel . . .

   _____happy_____.

   And I choose to . . .

   _____express it but control it_____.

2. You are playing during recess outside with friends. You notice two older boys tease and push a student. You see this student begin to cry and . . .

   In this moment, I feel . . .

   _____angry_____.

   And I choose to . . .

   _____stand up for him_____.

3. It is your first night at camp. The sky is starry and the moon is full. You hear the sound of frogs croaking and . . .

   In this moment, I feel . . .

   _____relaxed_____.

   And I choose to . . .

   _____lay down_____.

Acting on My Feelings

Here are two stories about two different kids who acted on their emotions.

A Bad Day for Chris

The day had started off miserably for Chris. First, he couldn't find the red belt for his team uniform. Then, one of the laces on his cleats broke. And finally, the new puppy had found his batting glove to be very tasty. Muttering loudly, Chris stomped his way to the dugout.

His coach walked up to him. "I see you are angry, Chris," the coach said. "When you're up to bat, focus on the ball. Put that energy into your swing, and get us a big hit!" And that's just what Chris did.

Rosalie and Her Grandmother

Before she died, Rosalie's grandmother often read to Rosalie from a special book of fairy tales. Rosalie loved the feeling of snuggling close to her grandmother while she read.

Sometimes, when Rosalie's mom was lonely for Grandmother, she would look at a photo album or play a special song on the piano. She seemed cheerier after that. So when Rosalie missed her grandmother, she knew just where she could find her—between the pages of a fairy-tale book.

> **This lesson will help you to:**
> - **explore** what influences your feelings.
> - **discover** how to express your feelings.
> - **make** a commitment to show respect toward yourself and others.

Think about a time when you acted on what you were feeling. How did you handle your feelings?

Catholics Believe

How do we know if our actions are right or wrong? God has given us a wonderful gift called our **conscience**. Our conscience works best for us when we train it to do a good job and then listen to it! We use the gift of our conscience as our guide in making good choices.

Ways to Show Feelings

Feelings themselves are neither good nor bad, right nor wrong. It is what we decide to act on that is important. Our actions, on the other hand, can be good or bad, right or wrong. Sometimes a wrong action—doing the wrong thing—makes us feel good. This does not make the action right.

Pretend you have won an award for the best school project. You feel joy and excitement! How do you show your feelings? You could happily say, "Thank you" to everyone who congratulates you. Or, you could go to the student who won the second place prize and say, "Ha, ha, I beat you!"

 You might enjoy both ways of showing your feeling of excitement. But only one way is the right way. Which is the right way? Why?

Feelings of Affection

Showing and receiving feelings of affection are very important actions. God blesses people with many ways to show true affection. One way to show affection is with words. You might say, "I like you" to a friend. Another way is through actions. You might give your mom and dad a hug. Married people show affection in special, private ways. This is a part of God's plan for family and for the creation of new life. As you grow older, your feelings of affection will change, and the words and actions you use to express those feelings will also change. Your words and actions should always be right for your age and proper between people.

Someone may tell you that the way she or he is treating you is meant to show you affection. This person may say things or try to touch you in ways that you know are wrong. These are not ways God wants affection shown. If this happens to you, you must make a courageous decision to say "No!" You should immediately get help from a family member or an adult whom you trust.

Growing in Virtue

Confidence is a virtue that can help you make good decisions and do the right thing even when it is difficult. With confidence you can try new things, or ask for help when you need it. We can act with confidence because we know that God is there to help us.

"Collage of Affection"

Look through magazines and newspapers for pictures of people showing affection as God intended. Cut out the pictures. Glue them in the space provided or on a separate sheet of paper. Add a title to your work.

Catholic Family Album

Saint Katharine Drexel was born in Philadelphia in 1858. Her family was very wealthy. She went to the best schools and traveled around the world. Katharine had great compassion and love for the poor. It took courage, but she told her family she wanted to care for people who needed help. Katharine Drexel spent her life serving Native American and African American people. She opened 50 missions for Native Americans in 16 states.

Showing Respect to All

To love as Jesus loves means to show respect for all people, not just the people who are easy to like. Showing respect means that we honor every person because they have been created in the image and likeness of God. We should love others because God loves them! When we respect a person, we treat that person as we would want to be treated.

On the lines below, write an action you could do that would show respect and love to each of the people listed. In the last space, add another person or two of your choice.

Person	Action That Shows Respect
Parents	hug them show a lot love
Sister/Brother	hug them shows love
Grandparents	hug them show a lot of love
Friend	talk to them saying
Teacher	listen
Neighbor	wave
Others	smile

Name ....

Summary

Remember what you have learned in each of the lessons in God's Gift of Self.

LESSON 3: My Feelings

- There are many types of emotions, and I can express them differently.
- Understanding how I feel can help me to make better decisions.
- I live the virtue of fortitude when I show strength in doing what is right.

LESSON 4: Acting on My Feelings

- I can learn how to act on my emotions through experience, advice and example.
- God gave me the gift of conscience to help me choose what is good and right.
- Because each of us has the dignity of being created in God's image and likeness, I am to respect myself and others.

Thinking It Through

1. What are some ways I act on my emotions?

when I'm happy I scream inside, when I'm sad I think about good things, When I'm mad I breath in and out.

2. What are the appropriate ways a person my age can express affection?

when they are happy or they can let out in their inside.

3. Imagine a world without mercy and forgiveness. What would it be like?

It would be boous

Choosing It Right

Circle the letter of the choice that best completes each sentence.

1. _____ is another name for the virtue of courage.
   a. Fortitude   b. Justice   c. Charity

2. You learn how to act on your feelings through experience, advice, and _____.
   a. thinking   b. television   c. example

3. Your words and actions should always be right for your age and _____.
   a. proper between people   b. pleasing to someone else   c. follow your feelings

4. Jesus shows us how to properly share our feelings with others because he is _____.
   a. only God   b. true God and true man   c. only human

5. When people are treated as if they have no value, we say they are _____.
   a. lucky   b. respected   c. abused

Name ....

Recalling Key Concepts

Circle the T if the statement is true. Circle the F if the statement is false.

1. Some feelings are right and some feelings are wrong.   T   F

2. People can react with different feelings to the same event.   T   F

3. Holding a grudge is a good way to act on your anger.   T   F

4. There are different kinds of affection.   T   F

5. Jesus acted on his feelings.   T   F

Fill in the missing words in these sentences.

6. If a person touches you in a way you know is wrong, you should
   say " .... !"

7. Your body and your .... work together to form
   emotions.

8. Various .... and certain people can trigger feelings.

9. God's gift of .... helps us to know and choose
   what is good and right.

10. We should show .... for all people.

Working Together

Music can influence our mood and shape our emotions. For this art project, you will need markers or crayons and some large drawing paper. Listen to three different types of music. While you listen to each, use colors and shapes to describe the mood you feel. Compare your three drawings with others in the class.

God's Gift of Life

Family Time

Family . . . Image of God's Life

God, who desired to share his love, created human life in his own image and likeness. To these human persons, the most wondrous of all his creatures, he gave the great responsibility to care for, to cherish and to protect all his creation.

The family is a profound image of God's own life, the life of the Holy Trinity. God lives and reveals himself in the ordinary and extraordinary, in the joys and the sorrows, in the challenges and struggles and everyday moments of family life. In our families, we learn the importance of caring for each other and for God's creation.

Influences all around us threaten to weaken and even tear apart the fabric of family life. Media and pop culture can invade our living rooms and challenge everything we believe to be true about life, and love and relationships. Yet, God's presence is constant, ever there, every day, in your family.

Healthy Habits in the Home

Evaluate your family's weekly activities. Does one person or a particular kind of activity dominate the schedule? When putting together the family schedule, be sure that everyone is included. Address the physical and spiritual health of the whole family.

Family Blessings

During family mealtimes this week, devote prayer to giving thanks to God for the gift of life. Ask that our culture be renewed in respecting and protecting life at every stage.

Taking the Lesson Home

Every stage of life offers opportunities to teach and to learn. Have each family member complete the sentences below.

See how many of these activities you can actually do.

1. I could teach a baby to . . .
   A baby could teach me to . . .

2. I could teach a teenager to . . .
   A teenager could teach me to . . .

3. I could teach a parent to . . .
   A parent could teach me to . . .

4. I could teach a grandparent to . . .
   A grandparent could teach me to . . .

Making Connections

You can learn a great deal about the sacredness of human life and the human body from your family. Ask family members the following questions and talk about their responses.

▶ What excitement and fear did you have about growing up when you were my age?

▶ How does our culture fail to show respect for the human body?

▶ How do we, as a family, show respect for the human body?

Faith on the Fridge

Christ has no body on earth but yours; no hands, no feet but yours. Yours are the eyes through which Christ's compassion for the world is to look out; yours are the feet with which He is to go about doing good; and yours are the hands with which He is to bless us now.

Saint Teresa of Jesus

Family Web Time
RCLBFamilyLife.com

Curious about Creation

Imagine a curious angel asking God about his creation of human beings.

Angel: Man and woman appear to be amazing creatures. What helps them do all that they can do?

God: I've given them both a body and a soul. The body has different systems that help them breathe, move, think, learn, feel, and enjoy life. Their bodily systems work together to keep them healthy.

Angel: How do these systems work?

God: There's a framework of bones and joints that holds the body together and helps the body move.

Angel: Do bones and joints move by themselves?

God: Oh, no. The muscular system makes every movement possible. The heart muscle pumps blood to the body. Muscles in the chest draw air into the lungs so the body can breathe.

Angel: Wow! Does something tell all of these systems how to work together?

God: Yes. There's a system that acts like a control center. The brain is in charge. It sends and receives messages through the spinal cord and billions of nerves. Tasting candy, feeling excited, and seeing colors all come from brain activity.

Angel: How will there be more humans?

God: Humans can share in my creation. I have created them with a reproductive system. A husband and wife can create a new human being called a baby.

Angel: The human body is quite amazing! You are a mighty Creator! You've thought of everything!

This lesson will help you to:

- **explore** God's plan in creating the human body.
- **discover** that God created you as a unique person.
- **make** the decision to deepen the respect for your body.

Why do you think it is important to know how your body works?

In Working Order

God created you according to a magnificent plan. He created you with a body and a soul. God desires you to be healthy and holy. As partially described in the dialogue between the angel and God, you learned that God created your body with many systems. In science class you can learn more about these individual body systems when you study biology and human anatomy. Here, you can learn that God created all of these body systems with an order, a particular way to help keep you healthy. When you are healthy, your body is working as God intended.

All of your body systems depend on each other to work properly. This is part of God's plan for your body. For example, your body cannot work without a digestive system. You need to eat food to sustain your energy. So God designed you with a system that includes your mouth, stomach, and small and large intestines—the digestive system. When you eat healthful foods, your digestive system can work its best. And when your digestive system is working its best, the rest of the body and its systems can work better too. The correct working order of your whole body is vital to your health.

 Imagine what you might do if one system wasn't working properly. For example, you become sick.

You can cooperate with God's plan for your body by choosing healthy habits. You can take the right steps for staying healthy, but sometimes you become sick due to no fault of your own. There are times when the body cannot be healed easily. This can be difficult, especially when the systems in the body are seriously damaged.

Your Unique Soul

The good news is that you are more than just your body. God created you with both a body and a soul. While your body is the physical part of who you are, you are much more. God created you with a soul, the spiritual part of you. Your soul is the innermost aspect of who you are. The soul is created immediately by God and is immortal. You are most especially created in God's image because of your soul. So even if your body is sick or damaged, you are not less of a person. For example, just because you need glasses to see, doesn't make you less of a person than someone who sees clearly. Some people, like doctors, study how God created the body to work. They search for ways to aid those parts of the body that aren't working properly. This is an amazing use of the minds and imagination God gave us.

Growing in Virtue

Being **healthy** means that our bodies are working as God intended. All four Cardinal Virtues (justice, fortitude, temperance and prudence) help us to show respect for ourselves when we maintain a healthy body and holy life.

"Systems in the Face"

Draw a profile of your face. Identify its major parts, and label each one with its body system name. For example, the mouth is part of the digestive system. In the skull or brain area, list some of the things your brain helped you remember, feel or learn today.

Choosing to Be the Wonderful You

Our bodies are the physical part of who we are. But, as amazing as our bodies are, we are much, much more! Remember that God created each of us with a soul, the spiritual part of us that never dies. God gave you a soul at the first moment of your life. You have God's life in you. It's a life that lasts forever.

Our bodies and souls work together. When we think and feel and choose, it is our soul active in us. We use our bodies to help us put these thoughts, feelings, and choices into action. Growing as followers of Jesus means growing in body and soul. Think about this amazing fact: no one else has ever been, or will ever be, exactly like you. You are God's unique creation.

Tell how you will respond, body and soul:

1. When I see someone who is sad, I will
   talk to them.

2. When I see or hear about someone in need, I will
   give them food.

3. When I see someone hurting another person, I will
   stop the person who is beating them up.

The Stages of Life

Growing Bigger and Stronger

Human life begins at conception. Conception is the joining together of a tiny egg cell from a mother and a tiny sperm cell from a father. This joining forms a new cell. With this unique cell, a new human life begins. This new human being grows quickly in the mother's womb for approximately nine months. While the baby is in the mother's womb, all of the major body systems begin to develop. For example, the baby's heart begins to beat as early as two weeks from conception. Right after birth, babies, called newborns, are very small and need special care.

The newborn quickly becomes an infant. The infant begins to learn about their world and family. The infant finds that milk fills the tummy and that hugs are good. During years one and two, toddlers are busy learning to walk and talk. They like to explore their world through their senses. Preschoolers are usually three to five years old. They can talk in sentences and learn how to play with others. They begin to learn to do many simple tasks.

Normally, when children are five or six years old, they are ready to go to school for a full day. This stage of life is called childhood. Children are still highly dependent upon their parents and other adults for many necessary things, such as food and shelter. They can also play sports and might have small jobs or chores at home.

You are now growing up in the last years of childhood. Soon you will be in your preteen years. Preteens are normally boys and girls not yet at the age of thirteen. After the age of thirteen, you will be a teenager. You will begin the stage of life called adolescence. As a teenager, you will continue to learn and develop as you grow bigger and stronger. At this point, you will be moving toward becoming an adult.

This lesson will help you to:
- **explore** the stages of human life.
- **recognize** the sacredness of life at every stage.
- **make** the decision to respect all life.

What is unique about human life at every stage?

The Stages of Human Life

All human life is sacred. Human life begins with a special act of love, the marital love of one man and one woman. Divine and human love create new life, a human person called a baby. Conception, pregnancy, and birth are part of the first major stages of life. More stages follow, such as infancy, childhood, and the preteen years. The major stages of life on Earth begin with conception and end in our bodily death.

Right now, you are just approaching the preteen years. Soon, you will leave childhood behind. You will become a preteen, then a teenager, and then a young adult. During all stages of life, the human person goes through many changes. These changes are physical, intellectual, emotional, and spiritual.

Preteens go through many changes, inside and out, especially when their bodies are reaching puberty. This is when a preteen becomes a teenager. At puberty, the bodies of boys and girls begin to develop to make it possible for them to have children one day. Once they become teenagers they will want to do many things for themselves. They will begin to make important choices with their parents about school, friends, and their future.

When people are in their twenties and thirties, they are called young adults. This is normally a time for making life-long commitments. Some young adults choose to remain single; others choose to be married. Some men and women enter the religious life; some men become priests. Those who enter the religious life or become priests do not marry. Priests and religious sisters and brothers care for the family of God, the Church.

As you grow older, you also grow in responsibility for your actions. Think about how you have matured in the last few months.

When people are in their forties and fifties, they are considered to be middle-aged adults. Many raise families. A married couple might be raising their children. They may be active in their career. This is a busy time of life. After all of this, some people enter retirement. Many retired people are elderly. This period of life can be a time for reflection. It is a time to share wisdom learned along the way.

Every person, no matter their age, is God's special creation. God is the author of all life. Every person gives us a glimpse of what God is like. Every human being at every stage of human life is sacred, or holy. When a human life ends on Earth, even though the body dies, the soul still lives. Jesus' Resurrection shows us we will live forever. God wants us to live with him, with Mary and with all the Saints in Heaven.

 Think about the qualities that each person in your family, young and old, share with the family. What is one thing each stage in the life cycle can offer to family life?

Growing in Virtue

The Theological Virtue of faith commits us to recognize that God created human life as sacred at every stage, from conception to natural death. **Sacredness** is the quality of being holy.

"The Cycle of Life"

Attach small pictures of people at all stages of the life cycle, from birth to old age to the spiral. Decorate it to symbolize the cycle of life.

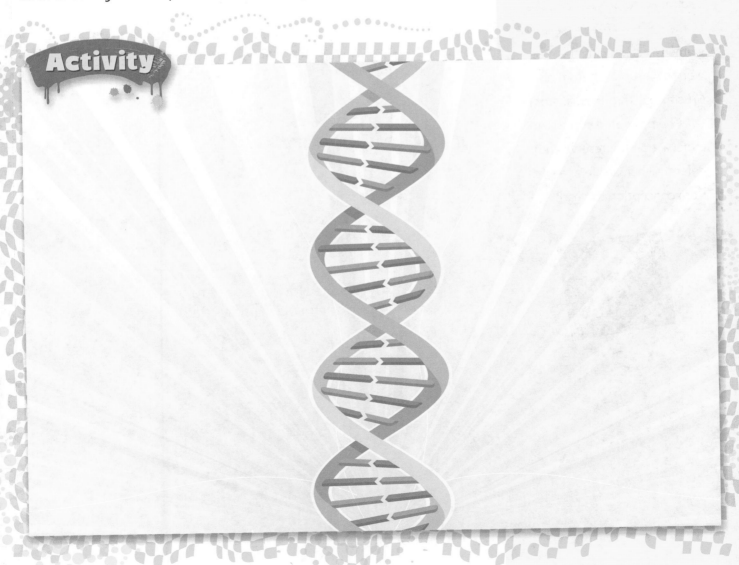

Activity

Building a Culture of Life

In the Dr. Seuss story, *Horton Hears a Who,* Horton, the elephant, becomes a hero. He responds to a cry for help from a tiny little person called a Who. Horton listened to the Who when no one else would. "Don't give up," he tells the Who. "I believe in you all! A person's a person no matter how small!" It is right to respect all creatures.

Every person, no matter how small, should be cared for and protected. When we care for and protect human life, we are building a culture of life. Every day, we can do more to show respect for every person. We can say "please" and "thank you" and "may I help you?" We can speak with respect to others. We can include those who feel alone. And we can listen to those who have no one to talk to.

1. Who are the people you know or have heard about who are just like the "Who"? Draw and label some of them.

2. Now be like Horton. Listen to the Who. Draw what you will do to show them you care.

here is warmth!

Name ....

Summary

Remember what you have learned in each of the lessons in God's Gift of Life.

LESSON 5: Your Amazing Body

- God created the human body with many systems.
- I can cooperate with God's plan for my body by choosing healthy habits.
- God created me with a soul from the first moment of my life.

LESSON 6: The Stages of Life

- Human life is sacred and begins at conception.
- The changes that I experience throughout my life are called the stages of life.
- Respecting every human person builds a culture of life.

Thinking It Through

1. What is the most important thing you can do to keep yourself healthy?

   Eat healthy.

2. What do you find exciting about growing up? What do you find scary?

   I find getting a job to be exciting but the scary part is doing alone, but with God but mostly alone

3. In what ways are you more than just your body?

   I am a soul.

Matching It Up

On each line, write the letter of the description in Column B that best goes with the term in Column A.

A

1. _D_ Conception
2. _A_ Infants
3. _E_ Teenager
4. _B_ Adulthood
5. _C_ Sacredness

B

A. Find that milk fills the tummy and that hugs are good
B. Normally a time of making life-long commitments and raising a family
C. The quality of being holy
D. When human life begins
E. After the age of thirteen, during adolescence

Name ....

Recalling Key Concepts

Circle the T if the statement is true. Circle the F if the statement is false.

1. Life begins at conception.   (T)   F

2. All of the human body systems work together to help a person live.   (T)   F

3. People stop learning when they are elderly.   T   (F)

4. God created us in such a way that we are more than our bodies.   (T)   F

5. Once you were born, you became a human being.   T   (F)

Fill in the missing words in these sentences.

6. You will soon be at the stage of life called ..... *preteen* ..... .

7. Choosing healthy ..... *not to choices* ..... is a way to cooperate with God's plan for your body.

8. God's gift of ..... *wisdom* ..... is sacred.

9. In the story, the angel told God that man and woman appear to be ..... *annoying* ..... creatures.

10. Your body, ... *spirit* ..... and ..... *soul* ..... work together.

Working Together

As a class, make life-size drawings of the body systems. Have your teacher choose the systems. Pick one group of students to work on each system. Now you are ready to begin. Place a large sheet of paper on the floor. Trace the outline of a classmate onto the paper. Cut out the shape of the body. Do this until you have one body cut out for each group. On the shape for your group, have someone draw the body system that you were assigned.

Family Time

Practicing Patience

Is everyone in your family happy with the age they are? Perhaps your child is thinking that they can't wait until they are old enough to do what their older brother or sister can do. Or perhaps you long for retirement.

The Vine Dresser & The Fig Tree
by James Tissot (1836–1902/French)

Share with your family the story that Jesus told about a man who planted a fig tree. Read the parable of the Barren Fig Tree in Luke 13:6–9. Help each family member understand that in this parable, Jesus is teaching us to be patient. He is telling us there are lots of good things about being your age.

There is another message in the story about the fig tree. Did the gardener sit around and do nothing? No. He gave the tree food and water to help it grow. Being patient doesn't mean sitting around and waiting for something to happen. It means doing things now to help build the future.

Healthy Habits in the Home

Talk to your family about patience. Make a list of some things that your family members hope for. What are some future goals for the family? Talk about ways to achieve these goals. Share some ideas about how to wait patiently.

Family Blessings

Have members of your family share significant happy times in their lives, especially times that they felt great affection and love for one another. Pray together, thanking God for the gift of love that is shared in your family.

Taking the Lesson Home

The more we understand the development of the unborn child, the more we can cherish God's gift of life in people at all stages. Families can show respect for life in many ways.

Find ways that are best for your family to:

1. support pro-life programs. Contact your local parish or diocesan pro-life, justice and peace, or mission awareness ministries

2. provide baby clothing to agencies, become a foster family, or offer financial support to homes for pregnant teenagers.

3. collect food, clothing, or money for the homeless in your community.

Making Connections

You can teach your child healthy and holy habits that show love. Discuss the following questions with them and talk about their responses.

▸ How do we as a family show patience toward one another?

▸ What will I do to guide my child to understand human sexuality?

▸ How can our good decisions show that we love one another?

Faith on the Fridge

True love between spouses is to be caught up in the love of the Trinity, strengthening each with grace so that their love may lead one another to God.

Based on *Church in the Modern World* 48

Family Web Time
RCLBFamilyLife.com

Growing and Maturing

Growing Over Time

Imagine looking at an album of photos taken of you before you were born. What do you think you would look like?

At the first moment of life, you were one tiny cell. A photo of you would have looked like a tiny dot. But that one cell quickly became two, then four, then eight cells. You kept on growing. Tiny as you were, God created you in such a way that one cell contained the plan for all your body systems. Scientists have discovered that this plan is found in your genes. Genes are found inside your cells. As these cells developed, your physical shape changed, just as it still does today.

Each cell "breathes," takes in food, gets rid of wastes, reproduces, and in time, dies. Cells have different shapes, according to the work they do. Some cells look like cubes; others look like rods, snowflakes, or even blobs of jelly. As you grow, your body adds more cells. By now your body has billions of cells. When you are an adult, you'll have trillions of cells.

Every person's body is made up of cells, but every person is different. God created you special. You are different in the way you look, think, and feel than every other person on Earth. God created you in his image and likeness. At each point and stage of your life you grow and mature in body and soul. You grow and mature both physically and spiritually. These changes are normal and natural. They are part of God's plan for you and for all people.

 What makes that very first cell of the human person so special?

This lesson will help you to:

- **explore** how humans grow over time.
- **discover** that growing and maturing as a person is a process that takes time and patience.
- **make** the decision to be patient and to keep your mind and heart open to God's presence while growing.

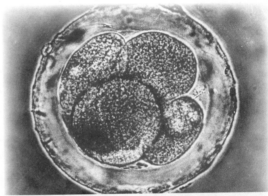

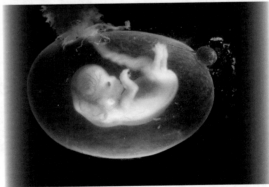

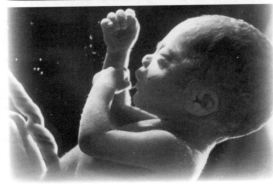

Growing in Virtue

Patience and self-control help us discipline ourselves. The habit of being able to wait and plan for things to happen in their proper time is patience. You need to practice patience as your body and mind grow.

At Their Proper Time

Growing up and becoming mature takes time. During this time of maturity you are growing physically, mentally, emotionally, and spiritually. God created you to grow over many years because things happen in their proper time. For example, you might have grown quicker than some of your friends. Or one of your friends might have figured out some difficult math problem quicker than you. And then again, you and your friends might all be wearing the same size sneaker. Either way, there is a proper time for things to happen for each person. And this is true for our families too.

Your family has changed and is still changing. Perhaps your family has changed because of a difficult situation. You might be asked to take on different responsibilities to help the family. Because you are taller and stronger than you once were, you can now help with more chores around your home. Perhaps your family has grown in size with new members. You might now be able to better help take care of them.

Think about how you and your friends have grown and changed over the years. How have you matured over this past year?

One sign of your maturing is visible in your ability to be patient. This can be very hard to do. Think of patience as a way to get yourself ready for something. Time is required for making plans, learning skills, and making friends. You need time to make plans so that things will happen at the right time and in the right way. If you want to play a sport, you need time to learn the skills, the rules, and the plays. Making new friends takes time and effort too.

As you learn how to care for yourself and others, you will find being patient helps things happen in their proper time. Being patient does not mean sitting around and waiting to get something you want. But it may mean getting ready to receive something you need. Getting ready includes having a pure heart. A pure heart is a heart open to receive what you need.

Maybe you want answers to questions you have about life, about family, about love, about being a good friend, about God. Keep an open and pure heart. Be patient and God will give you what you need to be the best person you can be for today and for tomorrow.

Learning to be patient helps you receive the gifts God has in store for you when you are ready!

Catholics Believe

Purity of heart builds on patience and is rooted in decency and good judgment. Having modesty guards a person from unloving and inappropriate acts.

"Growth Indicators"

Think about some of the times in your life when you would say, "Wow, I've grown!" or someone who knows you well would say, "Wow, you've grown!" Think about how you have grown—as a whole person. Name some of the times, ways and signs of your growth below.

Times and Ways I Have Grown

1 year old

5 years old

10 years old

Signs of My Growth

mean, less mean, nice

Catholic Family Album

Saint Monica was born in the early 4th century in northern Africa. Her husband was not a nice person, and her son, Augustine, didn't always behave very well. Monica prayed non-stop that her whole family would live holy lives. Her husband turned to God as he was dying. And Augustine became a Christian too. He is now known as one of the Church's greatest Saints, Saint Augustine of Hippo. Saint Monica had great trust in God, and she had patience.

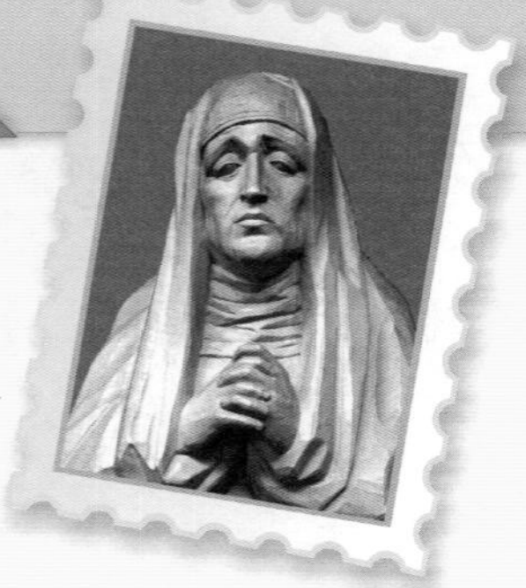

Helping Myself Grow

Growth can be fun and scary at the same time. Growth can take place on the inside and on the outside.

When you learned how to ride a bicycle without training wheels, you probably felt more confident. When that happened, you grew on the inside.

Jesus grew, too. He learned carpentry from his father. Learning how to cut wood must have been fun, but probably scary, too. That was growth. Jesus also learned about his faith, the Jewish law, and about trusting others. That was also growth.

Think about how you can help yourself grow. In the spaces below, tell what you can and will do to help yourself grow.

Healthy Discipline

You Have a Choice

"I'm quitting smoking!" Uncle Ted announced proudly.

"That's great," Marcus said, giving his uncle Ted a little nudge in the shoulder. "What made you decide?"

"I've realized that I need to feel better. I know I have an addiction. There are many chemicals in cigarettes that make it very hard for me to stop smoking. These chemicals give me a strong desire to keep smoking. So it's not going to be easy to quit. I wish I had never started. But quitting is the best decision I've made in a long time. It's a choice I'll be happy to live with and a choice that will help me live longer."

Becoming an adult may seem a long time away. But the decisions you make at your age will carry over to the decisions you make in the years to come. Now is the time to develop good habits. You always have a choice to act in a healthy and holy way.

You can choose to make healthy choices. You can say "no" to things that will harm you. You can say "no" to habits that are bad for you. You do not have to lie to a friend. You do not have to cheat on a test. You do not have to do anything that you know is harmful for you or to you. It can be difficult to say "no," especially to something you want or to someone you like. But you can make choices. You can have control over your actions.

You can say "yes" to habits that are good for you. You can brush your teeth after meals. You can wash your clothes. You can keep your body clean. You can exercise to stay fit. And you can pray for God's mercy, forgiveness, and grace to give you strength. You can choose to do good. You can live a life of healthy discipline.

This lesson will help you to:

- **explore** habits to keep your body and soul healthy.
- **discover** choices you can make to be healthy in body and spirit.
- **make** a decision to control your actions and live as a disciple of Jesus.

What are some choices you can make that will keep you healthy and holy?

Catholics Believe

The Great Commandment teaches us to love God and to love everyone as we love ourselves. We live the Great Commandment when we take good care of our mind, body, and spirit.

Developing Healthy Habits

How can you be as healthy and holy as God wants you to be? One way is to discipline yourself. This means to be in control of what you do and the choices you make. For example, you show discipline and self-control when you take care of your body and develop healthy habits. You also show discipline in the way you care for and use God's gifts of creation.

God gave you your life, and he wants you to enrich it, love it, and take care of it. To help do this, there are many healthy habits you can develop. You can eat right, exercise, and get the right amount of sleep.

Eating Right

To take care of your body properly you need to nourish your body. You need to practice the good habit of eating a balanced diet. Think of your body as a car that needs fuel to run. But unlike a car, your body needs several kinds of fuel to keep all of its systems working well. This fuel for your body is called nutrition. The energy you need to be active and healthy is your calorie need. Without good nutrition, your body can become weak and sick.

Nutrition experts have developed an "Eating Right Pyramid" to help people eat a balanced diet. For example, choosing and balancing the right amounts of foods from each part of the pyramid will give you the carbohydrates you need for energy. It will also give your body the protein it needs for building strong muscles and the vitamins and fiber you need for digestion. When you eat a balanced diet, you also give your body the calcium it needs to build strong bones and teeth.

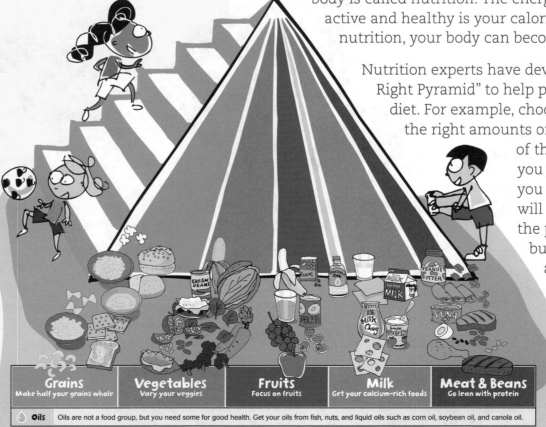

Grains — Make half your grains whole

Vegetables — Vary your veggies

Fruits — Focus on fruits

Milk — Get your calcium-rich foods

Meat & Beans — Go lean with protein

Oils — Oils are not a food group, but you need some for good health. Get your oils from fish, nuts, and liquid oils such as corn oil, soybean oil, and canola oil.

★ Find your balance between food and fun   ★ Fats and sugars — know your limits

Staying Active

The good habit of exercising every day, for example playing ball, riding a bike, dancing, hiking with your family, and other fun activities will help your heart and lungs, your digestion, and your spirit. A person is never too young or too old to develop the habit of being physically active every day.

Getting Enough Rest

The average fourth grader has a very busy day. At the end of the day, your body needs a break! Without enough sleep, your body is more likely to get sick, and you're more likely to be tired, cranky, and unable to think clearly. Remember, your brain needs a break, too!

God created you in such a way that your actions affect your health, physically and spiritually. Taking care of your body is a way of showing you're grateful for God's gift of life. Through practicing the good habit, or virtue, of temperance, you take care of your body, mind, and spirit. Taking care of yourself is a great way to love and respect yourself and God.

Growing in Virtue

Temperance is one of the four Cardinal Virtues. It is the virtue of self-control and discipline. Temperance helps you know how much is too much—whether it be food, play, or even work! Temperance helps us choose healthy and holy habits.

"Time to Keep Fit"

Get into small groups. Complete the chart below. Then discuss ways that the group can help each other keep fit. Report your results to the rest of the class.

Activity

Name	Hours of Sleep	Minutes of Physical Activity

Discipline in Action

Living a healthy and holy life takes work. We need discipline, which means having self-control. It helps us choose the habits that will keep us healthy and holy. Perhaps you have noticed that the words "disciple" and "discipline" are very similar. Disciples of Jesus always strive to imitate Jesus' words and actions. Being a disciple takes discipline!

Jesus taught us many ways to work toward a healthy and holy life. We call some of these the Corporal and the Spiritual Works of Mercy. These disciplined actions provide us a way to love others as God loves us. Each of these actions allows us to be a gift to another person in a loving way. Most of the Corporal Works of Mercy can be found in Matthew 25:34–40. Choose one of each and tell how you will put it into action.

1. **Corporal Works of Mercy**

   Shelter the homeless

   ~~prison the~~ visit the imprison

   I will _shelter the homeless and_

2. **Spiritual Works of Mercy**

   Counsel the doubtful

   forgive others

   I will _counsel the doubtful and_
   forgive others

Name ....

Summary

Remember what you have learned in each of the lessons in God's Gift of Love.

LESSON 7: Growing and Maturing

* Just as my body grows, I, as a whole person, am growing and maturing.
* Practicing patience can help me let things happen in their proper time.
* Keeping an open and pure heart helps me be ready to receive what God has in store for me.

LESSON 8: Healthy Discipline

* The healthy choices that I make can lead to healthy and holy habits.
* Showing discipline in the use of God's abundant gifts is a sign of love.
* I can offer myself as a gift to others by doing Works of Mercy.

Thinking It Through

1. What is the most important choice that I can make to keep myself healthy?

Eat healthy foods.

2. When is it most difficult for me to be patient? What can I do to become more patient?

When someone is playing I can ~~have fun~~ about cool things

3. How can I work on being a gift for others in a loving way?

Be very nice to them.

Choosing It Right

Circle the letter of the choice that best completes each sentence.

1. Some people develop _____ that are bad for them.
    a. smoking   (b.) addictions   c. praying

2. Jesus taught us many ways to work toward a healthy and holy life. We call these the _____.
    a. Works of Mercy   (b.) Healthy Choices   c. Balanced Diet

3. One tiny cell at the beginning of your life contained _____.
    a. food   (b.) your genetic plan   c. body systems

4. The energy you need to be active and healthy is your _____ need.
    a. sleep   (b.) calorie   c. virtue

5. Nutrition experts developed the _____ Pyramid to help people eat a balanced diet.
    (a.) Nutrition   b. Eating Right   c. Health

Name ....

Recalling Key Concepts

Circle the T if the statement is true. Circle the F if the statement is false.

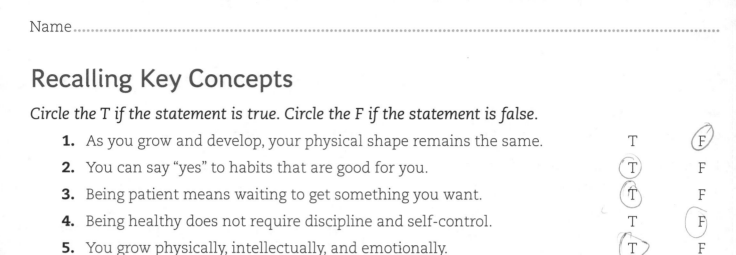

1. As you grow and develop, your physical shape remains the same.   T   (F)
2. You can say "yes" to habits that are good for you.   (T)   F
3. Being patient means waiting to get something you want.   (T)   F
4. Being healthy does not require discipline and self-control.   T   (F)
5. You grow physically, intellectually, and emotionally.   (T)   F

Fill in the missing words in these sentences.

6. You can pray for God's mercy and ....*forgiveness*.... to give you strength.

7. Growth can be ....*happy*........... and scary at the same time.

8. ....*You*............. is a character strength that helps discipline our actions.

9. Saint Augustine's mother, ...*St.*..... .....*Monica*..., prayed for his conversion.

10. ....*Health*......... is the Cardinal Virtue of moderating what you want with patience and self-control.

Working Together

Prepare a program for first graders on how to eat well. Bring foods that are healthful and explain why they are good for them to eat. Tell them why it is important to eat a variety of healthful foods every day. If possible, demonstrate good habits, such as how to be patient and disciplined when sharing a meal.

God's Gift of Community

Called to Charity

Following the Nazi invasion of Poland in the late 1930s, Maximilian Kolbe was arrested along with fellow Franciscan brothers. They were eventually released. Despite their hardships, Maximilian and his group helped Polish refugees, many of whom were Jewish. In 1941 he was arrested again and sent to the prison camp in Auschwitz. This time, despite torture and malnutrition, he ministered to the prisoners by hearing confessions and celebrating Mass. In July of 1941, Maximilian volunteered to take the place of Francis Gajowniczek, a married man with children who was to be murdered by the Nazis as retribution for other escaped prisoners. In 1982 the Church, under Pope John Paul II, officially recognized Maximilian Kolbe as a Saint, declaring him a martyr of charity.

You don't need to be a martyr like Saint Maximilian Kolbe to help others. Others need you in little ways every day. We are all called to speak out against the things that hurt people. We are all called to care for others and to help them during difficult times in their lives.

Healthy Habits in the Home

Evaluate the family's involvement in your parish's outreach ministry programs. What additional time, talent, or treasure can you and your family offer in support of these ministries?

Family Blessings

During family prayer, give attention to those who are excluded in our world. Provide an opportunity for each family member to share a name of someone whom they would like remembered as one in need of feeling accepted.

Taking the Lesson Home

Plan an activity that you can do with your family and friends. Keep it simple. The enjoyment will come from simply being together.

To plan an informal gathering of family and friends:

1. Let each member of the family choose a friend to invite.

2. Gather at your home or a nearby park.

3. Let the family prepare the meal.

4. Be sure to include a game or activity in which each friend can participate.

5. Prepare for alternatives in case of inclement weather.

6. Remember to keep it informal and casual.

7. Enjoy simply being together.

Making Connections

Learning to get along with others is very important. Sometimes it is hard to accept every person just the way they are. Ask family members and close friends of the family the following questions. Talk about their responses.

▶ Who do we know who has been excluded? How might we help them?

▶ What gifts do we see in one another? How do we show appreciation for these gifts?

▶ To other family members or friends: How did you know that God called you to the priesthood? To the religious life of a sister or brother? To the single life?

Faith on the Fridge

O Immaculata, our most loving Mother, we humbly implore you to take us, all that we are and have, wholly to yourself as your possession and property. Please make of us, our whole life, death and eternity, whatever most pleases you. For you obtain the grace of conversion and growth in holiness, since it is through your hands that all graces come to us from the most Sacred Heart of Jesus. Amen.

Based on Saint Maximilian Kolbe's Immaculata Prayer

Family Web Time
RCLBFamilyLife.com

Reaching Out

Left Out

Nine-year-old Anna was anxious to get to school. She was at a new school and still in the process of making friends. She wanted to talk with some of her new friends before school began.

As Anna entered the classroom, she saw Beth, Rachel, and Sue talking in the back of the room. Anna waved and walked over to them. They had done a science project together the day before.

"Are you wearing your play clothes to school?" Rachel asked Anna. Rachel giggled and pointed to a patch sewn on Anna's pants.

"No," said Anna, as her face turned red in embarrassment. "My three skirts were all in the laundry."

"Only three skirts?" mocked Sue. "You were right, Rachel. She really is poor," Sue continued.

"I'm sorry that you're poor, Anna," Beth said.

Sue then held up two pink envelopes with invitations to her birthday party. "Since you live in another part of town, I didn't invite you to my birthday party," Sue said to Anna while she gave one to Beth and the other to Rachel.

Anna felt so many things all at once. She was embarrassed and angry. She wanted to be friends with these girls, but at the same time, she didn't want their kind of friendship. They said she wasn't good enough to be with them. Anna's eyes filled with tears. She ran out of the classroom into the girl's restroom across the hall.

> **This lesson will help you to:**
>
> - **explore** how to welcome those who are different from yourself.
> - **discover** how to show acceptance of others.
> - **make** the decision to follow the Great Commandment and the Golden Rule.

 How can you include others in your community?

Catholics Believe

Love of neighbor is inseparable from love for God. Every community, with the aid of God's grace, is to support each person within that community by living the virtues.

You Belong in Community

Often a person is excluded from groups because of their differences. This happened to Anna because her neighborhood and clothes were different from the other three girls. Some people are excluded because of their skin color, culture, or gender. People with disabilities are often excluded because they see, hear, move, or act in a different way. When this happens, they are treated with prejudice. Treating a person with prejudice is wrong. It does not respect the dignity of a person.

Sometimes people are excluded from a group through teasing. Teasing is the act of annoying, bothering, or making fun of a person. Teasing might seem like innocent fun to some people. But teasing is wrong, and it can hurt the heart of another person. If you tease someone, you are deliberately choosing to tell that person that you do not want them in your group. Teasing a person is like slamming the door on someone who is ringing your doorbell. It is an act of disrespect.

Jesus never shut doors on anyone. He invites everyone to be his disciple and to belong to the Church. When Jesus was forming his group of friends, his disciples, and the Apostles, he welcomed many different kinds of people. He especially welcomed those who others excluded from their groups. He made friends with people who were less fortunate than others. By welcoming others with respect, you act the same way Jesus did in the way he treated all people.

How have you welcomed someone different from yourself? Think about ways that you can be accepting of people who seem different.

When people become friends, or form a community of friends, they often have things in common. But friends also enjoy learning about their differences. You can welcome those your age into your group of friends. You can welcome those who have things in common with you as well as those who are different from you.

Think of your group of friends as a community. Look carefully at the word "community" and notice that the letter "u" is in the middle. Seeing that "u" in the middle says a lot. You belong in the middle of a community. Accepting someone as a friend means that you respect that person. Your words and actions show that he or she belongs in the community.

Growing in Virtue

Prudence is the skill of knowing what is right. It helps a person consistently make good judgments. Accepting others as a part of the community is respectful and right.

"Same but Different"

In the space provided, complete both sides. On the left side, write the ways in which you think you are like other people. On the right side, list the ways you think you are different.

Activity

Ways that I'm like other people . . .	Ways that I'm different from other people . . .
I like to play	I don't
I like to watch movies	I don't
I like ice cream	I don't
I like to play video games	I don't
I like to talk with people	I don't

Catholic Family Album

Blessed Teresa of Calcutta was born Agnesë Gonxhe Bojaxhiu in 1910 in Albania. Agnes was passionate about missionary work and took her religious vows in 1937 taking the name, Teresa after Saint Thérèse of the Child Jesus. By 1950 she had formed her own community, the Missionaries of Charity, to serve the poor, particularly in India. Mother Teresa believed that with a pure heart you could see God in every person. She once said, "Love does not measure, it just gives."

Putting Others First

We sometimes feel like treating others in a way that we know is not caring. When this happens, we are being tempted not to live as Jesus taught us to live. Jesus teaches that we are to love God and our neighbors, even those who we do not like or understand. We are not to be mean or selfish. This way to love is called the Great Commandment. It says: "You shall love the Lord, your God, with all your heart, with all your soul, and with all your mind. . . . You shall love your neighbor as yourself" (Matthew 22:37–39).

Jesus also taught an important rule called the Golden Rule. He said, "Do to others whatever you would have them do to you" (Matthew 7:12). You show love by caring for others through your thoughtfulness. A thoughtful person thinks about the needs of other people. You can practice the Golden Rule by trying to put yourself in another's place and thinking about how you would like to be treated.

You know types of people who are not always treated with respect. List these people in the chart below. Then decide on actions that you will take to show them you care.

People who are not treated with respect:

_____
_____
_____
_____
_____

How I will show that I care:

_____
_____
_____
_____
_____

In Little Ways

A little over one hundred years ago, a French girl at the age of fifteen was sure of how she wanted to show her love for God. She wanted to honor God with great love. She begged the Pope in person to let her become a nun even though she was only fifteen. Soon, Thérèse Martin entered the Carmelite Convent in Lisieux and became a Carmelite nun.

Thérèse was an ordinary girl from a small town in France. Her life was not easy. She suffered from bad headaches and fevers, and it was hard for her to sleep. But Thérèse didn't let these things stop her from doing God's work. She realized that she did not have to do great things to serve God, the nuns in her community, and other people. Doing little, ordinary things were Thérèse's way of doing God's work.

Thérèse knew in her heart that God was calling her to love him by helping others. Every day she found little "ordinary" ways to love God. Sometimes this meant being patient and kind to the sisters in her convent who were hard to get along with. When Thérèse was sick or tired, she would pray the Lord's Prayer and the Hail Mary very slowly. Saint Thérèse prayed in her own little way.

Thérèse died at the age of twenty-four. Her last words were said to be, "My God, I love you!"

? *What are some of the little ways you can show your love for God?*

> **This lesson will help you to:**
>
> - **explore** a life of virtue needed to love God.
> - **discover** the different ways people can serve God.
> - **make** a decision to care for the world.

A Call for All

Thérèse knew that God created each of us to know, love, and serve him, and to love other people as we love ourselves. Thérèse discovered ordinary ways of serving others to show her love for God. This was her vocation. A vocation is a call from God to live a certain way. You might think of the word "vocation" as the way you are going to love your way through life. Your life is an adventure of discovering how you will love God by serving others.

Thérèse discovered that her vocation was to the religious life in the community of the Carmelite sisters. Because of her great love for God, the Church has named Thérèse a Saint and a Doctor of the Church. Many other women have joined religious orders and communities approved by the Church. Members of religious communities love God by serving others. Men can become religious brothers, or deacons, or they can become priests. Religious brothers often serve as teachers or missionaries. The priesthood is a service to God and to the Church.

 Think about one or two of your gifts. What are they? How do you use them?

There are other ways in which we can love our way through life. Single persons also have a special vocation. They can use their gifts in service of God and others in many ways. God also calls some people to the married life. In marriage, wives and husbands show their love for God by loving and serving each other. They support each other as they join together to have a family.

God calls each person to a vocation and gives each person the gifts to live out that vocation. Our job is to discover what our gifts and vocation are and then choose to use them to love God and serve others. Now is a good time to focus on your gifts. You probably have an idea of what some of them are. Use them. What you decide to do as a grown-up will depend on the talents and abilities you develop now.